Ginger Rogers
& Fred Astaire

A Biography

Katy Holborn

Copyright © 2017.

Table of Contents

Movie Magic

What makes a person a star?

This is one of the greatest mysteries of the entertainment world. How can someone be propelled from an ordinary existence into the extraordinary, lifted from the Earth and soaring into the stratosphere?

Like lightning caught in a bottle, some people have that certain X-factor in their bodies and personalities. They manage to house the mysterious "It" that encapsulates the needs and desires of a large mass of people at a particular point in time.

These people are stars.

But as surely as stars rise, most also fall. They wax and wane, and vanish into the annals of history, touching and brilliant, but only for a time.

A few, however, do not fade. Their names and faces become unforgettable, seeping into the lifeblood of popular culture. Timeless and iconic, they remain relevant and inspirational even to a changed world.

Fred Astaire and Ginger Rogers are two of these undying stars, amongst the greatest figures of Hollywood's Golden Age.

Fred and Ginger together was pure, perfect alchemy. They transformed matter into cinema gold and became the most memorable dance partners in movie history.

Another Hollywood legend, Katherine Hepburn, once famously said of the pairing: *"He gave her class and she gave him sex appeal..."*

It was one way of attempting to understand how, out of so many other people who could have matched either of them, this pair somehow worked.

Together, they turned supporting parts into scene-stealing roles. With their bodies, they translated sound and feeling into dance, and in a single breathtaking sequence can tell elaborate stories of flirtation, sensuality and love.

Their magic kept their fledging studio, RKO, afloat during tough financial times – a studio that would later be able to release what is regarded as the greatest movie of all time, *Citizen Kane* (1941). The pair also wowed American audiences during the Great Depression – raising up spirits and spinning dreams as they glided across the dancefloor.

Hollywood's Golden Age

There are conflicting accounts of what chronological period precisely defines "Hollywood's Golden Age."

Some say it began at the decline of the silent movie era while others include it – after all, that period of filmmaking from the 1910s to the 1920s saw the unforgettable Charlie Chaplin making waves nationwide, and the formation of many of the major movie studios: Universal (1912), Paramount (1916), United Artists (1919), Columbia (1920), Walt Disney (1923), Warner Brothers (1923), MGM (1924) and RKO (1928).

Whichever point of beginning one chooses to believe, what is certain is that The Golden Age of Hollywood was a time of change, experimentation, the introduction of bold technologies and products, and of course, growth in output and reach of the movie industry.

The foundations over which the gargantuan American cinema would stand and remain dominant in the World, were established in this heady period.

Perhaps the most transformative change to occur at this time was the decline of silent films and the rise of "Talkies." While silent films did come with music when watched in the cinema, talkies synchronized visuals and audio on the screen. After *The Jazz Singer* (1927) came out, Hollywood was never quite the same again.

Not that it was the first piece of film with synchronized audio and visuals. Warner Brothers, for example, had already achieved some success in the endeavor earlier the decade for short films. But *The Jazz Singer* (1927) is the most notable marker that separated the silent film era, from the talkies that followed after it.

It was a financial success even with limited showings (not a lot of theaters had the necessary equipment to show it properly). Cinemas were packed, and where there is demand – supply usually follows.

Everyone had to adjust to this new incursion into their Hollywood lives. To be able to meet the demand for talkies, studios had to invest in both equipment and stages, as well as in their actors.

Many actors took not only lessons to improve their speech, but also had to adjust their style of performance. There was now less pantomime and exaggerated expressions that were friendlier to silent film, and more restrictive movement so as not to disturb hidden microphones and sensitive sound capturing equipment. Speaking accents had also become a problem for actors, who found their roles limited if they were unable to adjust according to the demands of a role.

Some actors either could not maintain or did not wish to maintain their standing in this changed industry. Some were old and already used to a certain way of doing things, and were prosperous enough to retire or move on to other things. Others returned to the stage. Some silent movie stars thrived of course – Greta Garbo's husky voice and Swedish accent matched her mysterious appeal, for example - but others fell away.

But with the synchronization of sound, there were also actors who were just waiting in the wings for their opportunity to shine.

RKO Pictures

As *The Jazz Singer* (1927) was taking the town by storm, Hollywood legend holds that two executives sat down to a meeting at New York Grand Central station's Oyster Bar to form RKO. These were David Sarnoff, president of RCA, and financier Joseph Kennedy (father of future U.S. President JFK).

Kennedy had recently bought Film Booking Offices of America ("FBO"), which distributed European films and American indies as well as ran a humble Hollywood production outfit. As for Sarnoff, he wanted to make headways into the movies with a new sound system, and had interest in FBO.

Together, they then turned their attention to acquiring a theater chain. This steered them toward the Keith-Albee-Orpheum vaudeville houses. Soon, they closed the deal and became RKO: Radio-Keith-Orpheum.

RKO had lofty ambitions as an entertainment conglomerate, with cards to play in the movies, on radio, and even international entertainment via the French outfit, Pathe.

It established itself as a major player right away, landing Broadway screen rights, hits, and production facilities. They also landed one of Hollywood's brightest executive talents: the wunderkind David Selznick, who was brought on board in 1931 to significant success.

He didn't stay long, reportedly besieged by conflicts on the upper echelons of studio management. He went on to thrive elsewhere though, while RKO struggled in the tumultuous financial burdens of the Great Depression.

But before Selznick left, he made many important moves that kept RKO above water. One of them was the signing of a certain Mr. Fred Astaire.

He Also Dances

The Great Depression was a long, deep and wide-scale economic downturn that impacted the United States and a lot of the industrialized world.

It ran from 1929 to 1939, and saw the stock market crash; wiped out many investors; felled companies which then laid off workers who then spent less; which in turn decreased demand and output... all in a dizzying tailspin of seemingly inescapable decline.

It was not a good time for plenty of Americans; at its worst, it is believed half of America's banks failed and 15 million citizens were unemployed. A lot of people went into debt, repossessions and foreclosures spiked, and many Americans barely had enough to scrape by.

Yet in the 1930s, attendance at the movies was estimated to be at 80 million weekly. Cinema proved to be a welcome diversion from all the hardships of life.

In movies there was adventure and escape, glamor and romance. And after the talkies revolution of the latter part of the 1920s, there was also a lot of music and of course, dancing. Some of the greatest dancing to be found on film, as a matter of fact, came our during those tough economic years.

One of the most compelling draws of Great Depression cinema, however, almost never came to be.

Frederick Austerlitz Takes the Stage

Before there was suave "Fred Astaire," there was a young boy named Frederick Austerlitz, born on the 10th of May 1899 in Omaha, Nebraska.

His parents were Frederic "Fritz" Austerlitz, an Austrian immigrant, and Johanna "Ann" Geilus, a second-generation Prussian-American. He had an older sister, Adele.

Young Frederick was a serious and somewhat frail child, and his parents hoped dance classes might build up his athleticism. He was enrolled at the local Chambers Dance Academy along with his older sister, who was believed to be the bigger talent.

Frederick did not take dance too seriously right away, while Adele was charismatic; a natural. Before long though, Frederick found his own way forward in a manner that, while different from Adele, became complementary to his sister's approach. She was intuitive, improvisatory and seemingly carefree. His approach was through innovation and perfectionism.

Adele was Fred Astaire's first partner, and the high benchmark after whom everyone to follow would compare.

The Austerlitz siblings impressed at the school, and their parents were encouraged to help them maximize their potential. And so, the brother-and-sister prodigies soon packed their bags and headed for the bright lights of New York City.

Their mom accompanied them and was also their tutor and manager. Their dad stayed at home in Omaha to look after the family business, the earnings from which helped support his wife and children as they pursued a career in New York. Expenses included securing the services of teachers and agents – expenses they would eventually be able to cover for themselves.

It was January 1905 when the three Austerlitzes took the train and their talents to the Big Apple... Adele was eight years old and her brother Frederick, just five.

In New York the duo found top-of-the line training and exposure to diverse forms of art and dance. There were also plenty of opportunities to perform. They paid their dues and played in recitals and amateur shows, eventually moving up to small-time vaudeville. They took their show to stops in the American heartland, before cracking the bigger cities. They started as openers, before climbing higher up the billing.

The Austerlitzes landed a contract with the Orpheum Circuit, which brought the young siblings' Vaudeville act all over the country. All throughout, they gleaned valuable skills, experience and professionalism, and made invaluable creative and professional connections.

Among the acquaintances they made over years in the industry were famed Spanish dancers Eduardo and Elisa Cansino, and the great Bill "Bojangles" Robinson – from whom young Fred picked up tap dancing. They also met and eventually worked with the iconic composer brothers, George and Ira Gershwin. Fred met them while they were also building their own legend.

Adele and Frederick's time as a duo established the future, signature look of Fred Astaire: dancing in top hat and tails. It is believed the top hat was a convenient way to mask his height when his older sister and dance partner was still taller than him. The grace, class and elegance the look would be associated with was almost secondary to its initial, practical purpose.

Like all child performers, however, Adele and Fred grew up, and it wasn't exactly good business for acts packaged as young prodigies. Their selling proposition began to weaken around 1909-1911. They needed to be beyond cute and prodigious – they had to be among the best. They had to deliver on the promises of their youth, in some of the most competitive artistic scenes in the world.

Fred, at 12 years old, buckled down. He took his craft more seriously and the duo improved and re-tooled, such that by mid-decade, the siblings were doing better than ever.

The siblings started going by "Astaire" in 1917 - their mom/manager reportedly felt their name "Austerlitz" sounded like a battle and championed the change. It was also around this time that the siblings became more impactful performers in the industry.

Beginning with the Shuberts' revue, *Over the Top* (1917), they found a lot of success in Broadway. The siblings were in this and several other revues and musical comedies for more than a decade.

There was a lot of work to be had in the Great White Way, there was good pay, and there was also family: the Astaires' father even got to join them in Manhattan by 1920 before he passed away.

Success in New York eventually brought them across the sea and into London stages. There, the siblings brought their act, and were beloved for successful runs of the hit show that made George and Ira Gershwin superstars, *Lady, Be Good*!

(1924 – 1925) and later, the Gershwins' *Funny Face* (1927 - 1928).

While the Astaire siblings were successful together, there was some consensus that Adele was the bigger draw. She - gamine, funny and charming on top of being talented - tended to get great notices. But Fred also started coming into his own.

In *Lady Be Good*, he had his first major solo and it was just as well too – the London shows brought Adele Astaire not only professional acclaim but romance and shortly after that... retirement. For many women at the time, marriage meant the end of the pursuit of a profession.

The siblings had heir final appearance as a professional duo in the critical and commercial hit revue, *The Band Wagon* (1931). Adele thereafter married Lord Charles Francis Cavendish, and she never graced the stage again.

As for the less flashy Astaire sibling...

Fred's successful turn in *The Gay Divorce* (1932 - 1933), the only Broadway show he went on sans his brilliant older sister, proved he could get by perfectly well on his own.

It wasn't an immediate hit. Some of the initial critical response was cutting and had pointedly noted the effects of the absence of flashy Adele, but Fred Astaire nevertheless managed to carry a hit show. He needed a bit of a romantic jolt, though. Long used to dancing with his sister, his partner for *the Gay Divorce*, glamorous Claire Luce, reportedly had to tease it out of him.

The *Gay Divorce* run also landed Fred Astaire hit songs on the radio. While Astaire may be more famous for dancing on film, it should be noted that he made hundreds of musical recordings over the course of his career. As a matter of fact, by the time he'd appeared in *The Gay Divorce*, he had already released several.

Fred has had recordings of music since the 1920s, when he was working with his sister Adele and songs from their shows would be recorded for release. He'd even had several solos by then.

Many of these songs were released before music charts were uniformly and widely established, but it is believed by researchers that plenty of Astaire records can be considered top 10 hits by today's measures. That was especially the case for the Cole Porter ballad, "Night and Day" from *Gay Divorce*. It is believed to have hit the equivalent of a number one by today's standards, and helped make the show the hit that it eventually turned out to be.

Thus, with *Gay Divorce*, Fred Astaire had not only a number one song, but a stage musical that played for 248 performances on the cutthroat world of Broadway.

Next, Fred turned his attention to motion pictures.

One studio seemed to be an especially ideal destination for a performer like Fred, who had a dance background, stage experience and Broadway connection: RKO Pictures.

RKO it may be recalled, was born in 1928 after the talkies. It did not have the thick silent movie histories of other studios and was open to experimentation, especially with sound. Because it was relatively new, it was also still looking for its identity and expertise. Furthermore, RKO inherited vaudeville theaters upon its formation. This studio, whether anyone really knew it at the time, was uniquely poised to absorb and magnify the talents of an artist like Fred Astaire.

But first, he had to go through a tough screen test. The verdict was unfortunately harsh. The precise words vary depending on the source of the report: *"Can't act. Can't sing. Balding. Can dance a little."* or *"Can't Act. Slightly Bald. Also Dances."*

Either way, the basic idea was the same.

As the legend goes, the opinion of the executive who made this evaluation was overruled by the great David O. Selznick before he left R.K.O. Selznick was reportedly floored by Astaire's dancing and his charm.

Thus, Fred Astaire landed his contract and made his way to Hollywood, in spite of the lukewarm reception to his initial screen test.

He started out on loan to MGM, via *Dancing Lady* (1933). The film starred Hollywood legends Joan Crawford and Clark Gable, and the debuting Fred Astaire was further down the bill. But he wouldn't be down there for very long.

On his very first outing with RKO, he had a character role in the lavish musical, *Flying Down to Rio* (1933).

Flying Down to Rio (1933)

The romantic comedy musical, *Flying Down to Rio* stars Dolores del Rio as an engaged Brazilian beauty; and Gene Raymond, as a flirtatious band leader who falls in love with her.

The movie and its stars were well-received, but the fourth and fifth-billed actors were scene-stealers: plucky actress Ginger Rogers and vaudevillian Fred Astaire. Sidekicks to the main show, they nevertheless stole hearts with a two-minute dance called "The Carioca." It became all the rage, and was their first steps toward a legendary partnership.

Interestingly, it actually wasn't the first time they danced together.

Earlier in the decade, they met on the New York stage. In 1930, Ginger was on the Broadway show, *Girl Crazy*, which featured music by George and Ira Gershwin. She was nineteen years old, working in both stage and screen but yet to be a major star.

Around this time, Fred Astaire was a stage veteran known for his dancing prowess. He was also a good friend and collaborator with the Gershwin brothers since they were teenagers and before stardom in 1916. Astaire was brought in to help Ginger and the other actors with choreography.

If the stories hold true, Ginger was in rehearsals for a routine with the song, "Embraceable You." Fred then asked her - "*try it with me.*"

At the time, no one really knew just how important this first dance was. What was clear though, was that *Girl Crazy* was a smash and that Ginger had star power. Soon after the show's triumphant run, she devoted herself more fully to the movies. She left the stage for Hollywood, and Fred Astaire wouldn't be her dance partner again for years.

Virginia Katherine McMath

Long before she formed half of one of Golden Age Hollywood's most beloved and unforgettable pairings, Ginger Rogers was born on the 17th of July, 1911 in Independence, Missouri.

She was the only child of electrical engineer William Eddins McMath, and his wife, the formidable and Lela Emogene Owens McMath (also known as "Lelee" or "Lela").

The McMaths married and became parents young. But even before Virginia was born, her mother Lela ran away from her husband. They eventually divorced and Lela made a living for herself and her daughter, as a reporter and screenwriter.

For a time, Lela had to leave young Virginia with family in Missouri. She became a scriptwriter in Hollywood under the name "Lela Leibrand." She later became a reporter for the U.S. Marines, and carried the distinction of being one of the first females joining the Marine Corps at the start of World War I.

A more stable family life came when Lela married insurance broker John Logan Rogers in 1920. The couple and young Virginia settled in Texas.

Virginia took her stepfather's last name, "Rogers," even if she was not formally adopted (and even if her mother would eventually part ways with John). The "Ginger" she would eventually be famous for has a different provenance. She landed it because one of her young cousins couldn't get around to saying "Virginia."

Ginger on the Rise

Amongst Lela's various professional writing jobs was a steady assignment covering theater. The beat brought her — and by her design, her daughter as well — in the path of many creatives.

This is just the first of many ways Lela became instrumental to shaping Ginger's career, though friends who knew the family in Texas claimed she was not pushy; Ginger ran on her own engine, and mother and daughter were very close.

Ginger was naturally bubbly and studied some dance in her youth, and eventually became a champion performer of the Charleston at the age of 14 in 1925.

Winning the Texas State Charleston Competition came with the prize of going on a professional touring circuit for four weeks. She, along with her now-manager mother, thus embarked on a new adventure.

In one iteration of Ginger's nascent stardom, she and Lela hired her competition runners-up as backing dancers to form a group known as "Ginger and Her Redheads." They were a crowd-draw, and their popularity helped extend the original four-week contract to six months.

Eventually though, Ginger became a solo act, showing off her talents in dancing and baby-talk monologues.

But she was not solo for long! She married a fellow vaudeville performer named Jack Culpepper in 1929. Ginger was 17 and he, 29 - it was a marriage in defiance of her mom Lela's wishes, but she was allowed to live and learn on her own. Together, Ginger and Jack were briefly known as the vaudeville act, "Ginger and Pepper."

"Ginger and Pepper" lasted only for a hot minute though, before the romance fizzled out. Jack was said to have had problems with drinking. The couple split after a few months (but wouldn't be divorced until 1931).

Ginger Rogers became a solo act with stints in St. Louis and Chicago. For the latter, she sang with an orchestra that had a tour stop in New York City – a place which took to her star potential quickly. She was discovered by a night club owner, who then brought her to the attention of the composers behind a Broadway production called, *Top Speed* (1929).

Her ascent to stardom suddenly accelerated in the Big Apple – it is unbelievably fitting that her first major break was for *Top Speed*, because that is precisely how her career progressed from there. Her performance garnered not only positive reviews – it also yielded a contract with Paramount Pictures.

And just like that, Ginger Rogers had Broadway credentials and a major studio contract, in basically the same year she married and separated, then moved to pursue stardom in New York City.

For a time, 19-year-old Ginger dabbled in both stage and screen. She also managed to work with major studios aside from Paramount Pictures, such as Pathe, RKO and Warner Brothers. She did bit parts alongside bigger roles going into the early 1930s, as she steadily built up her body of work.

Ginger had small parts in the short films, *A Day of a Man of Affairs* (1929); *Campus Sweethearts* (1930); and *A Night in a Dormitory* (1930). But she also had better exposure for films from the same period, like *Office Blues* (1930); and her feature debut, *Young Man of Manhattan* (1930) with Claudette Colbert. With these and many other films, she was a busy young actress with a lot of promise.

Her first big break, however, came on the stage: she was cast in the Gershwin musical, *Girl Crazy* (1930).

It was here that she first worked with stage veteran, Fred Astaire, during rehearsals. Even more importantly though, her talents and presence commanded wider attention. After *Girl Crazy*, she left theater for a while for better focus on the movies. Naturally, her next destination after New York was Hollywood.

The Road to *Rio*

Fred Astaire and Ginger Rogers are beloved figures of the Hollywood Golden Age, both as a duo and as individual artists. There are, however, some people who undervalue what Ginger brought into the pairing versus what Fred had.

He was the more experienced and technically skilled dancer, the older and more seasoned performer, the male lead, and a co-choreographer with a bent for perfectionism and control… hallmarks of a great and hardworking talent indeed.

But what fans of Rogers and modern-day feminists romantically note is this: Ginger could do what Fred could do… in heavy gowns, in high heels, and backwards.

She was also an ambitious and accomplished performer in her own right. As a matter of fact, by the time they appeared on screen together for the first time in *Flying Down to Rio* (1933), she had already been in about 19 movies prior, versus his 1. A good number of these pre-pairing films were not only hits, they also became important movies for American cinematic history. Among them:

***Young Man of Manhattan* (1930).** Before Ginger Rogers' landmark partnership with Fred Astaire was launched by *Flying Down to Rio* (1933), she had a memorable role in *Young Man of Manhattan* (1930). As a plucky Jazz Age flapper, she delivered a catchy quip that became one of the most popular at the time: "*Cigarette me, big boy!*" It was a pop cultural feat, in a year where she appeared in four full-length movies (aside from appearing in several short films).

***Gold Diggers of 1933* (1933).** While not all of her projects were as memorable or impactful, Ginger was a prolific actress and continued doing movies in 1931 and 1932, until she found a set of particularly iconic roles: in *Gold Diggers of 1933* (1933) and *42nd Street* (1933) for Warner Brothers.

These movies are considered to have put her firmly on the Hollywood map.

In the Depression-era film, *Gold Diggers*..., she captured the zeitgeist in the opener, where she appeared in a costume made of gold coins while singing, "We're in the Money." She memorably performed part of it in Pig Latin. If the stories hold true, she was heard playing around with it on set and the director decided to add it into the scene.

The film wasn't just a hit when it came out; over time, it was deemed historically and culturally significant enough for preservation. *Gold Diggers of 1933* is in the National Film Registry of the Library of Congress.

***42nd Street* (1933).** In the single year that *Gold Diggers of 1933* came out, Ginger Rogers was in ten films. One of these was Academy Award Best Picture nominee, *42nd Street* (1933). Like *Gold Diggers...*, it was a dazzling musical about the backstage goings-on of a Broadway show. Also like

Gold Diggers..., *42nd Street* was important to American film beyond just grossing well.

It is in the National Film Registry too, showing it stands the test of time. It also helped popularize the backstage narrative so beloved and now so familiar in cinema, and has such enduring appeal it made its way into Broadway stages several times, to Tony Award-winning glory.

The film was also groundbreaking for its extravagant, large-scale dance numbers that were choreographed by the legendary Busby Berkeley (who had also worked on *Gold Diggers...*). His lavish vision and inventive use of available cinema technology created dazzling scenes of unforgettable, signature mass choreography. He was a genius at finding fresh ways to bring the art of dance into the big screens. The film was such a hit that it helped stave off the financial woes of its studio, Warner Bros., when it was released.

As sassy chorus girl "Anytime Annie," Ginger was very much a part of the movie's mass appeal. It was a substantial role in a big movie, but Ginger was meant for even greater things, especially after all her efforts led to a signing with RKO.

But 1933 was an eventful year for the young actress not only in terms of career but also for her personal life. She appeared on the film, *Don't Bet on Love* (1933) with the boyishly handsome actor, Lew Ayres, who would later be her second husband.

Lew Ayres. Ayres made his mark in Hollywood in 1930, as the star of the acclaimed war film, *All Quiet on the Western Front* (1930).

Ginger is said to have harbored a soft spot for him since seeing the movie, and they fell in love in 1933 and wed in November, 1934. Ginger and Lew were married from then to 1941, though they separated before they divorced.

This marriage lasted longer than Ginger's first, but it was her partnership with another Hollywood actor at this same period, which became far more popular and enduring...

Some people even wondered if they were in love.

Shall We Dance?

As was mentioned earlier, Fred Astaire and Ginger Rogers have danced together before, on the Broadway stages for rehearsals of *Girl Crazy* (1930) in New York. But it was in their films for the studio, RKO, where they attained their legend.

It was an unlikely beginning. *Flying Down to Rio* (1933), the first film they appeared in together, was supposed to be the vehicle for another star, the beauty, Dolores del Rio. And while their roles were prominent, Ginger and Fred were supporting characters on the fourth and fifth billing. Furthermore, Ginger was not even supposed to be in the film; she was the replacement for a different actress.

Fred Astaire played sidekick to the leading man, and both men were members of a band whose vocalist was played by Ginger Rogers. The actress originally slated for the role was Dorothy Jordan, who stepped back from the project after marrying and going on her honeymoon.

And so the role went to Ginger, an RKO talent and veteran of 19 films, who had already been in two important musicals previously. It was also advantageous that she had previously worked with Fred.

But the supporting actors somehow became scene-stealing crowd-pleasers in the film, and they seemed to capture the needs and wants of the filmgoing public at the time.

Together, Fred and Ginger electrified the screen with their infectious energy, everyman appeal and undeniable chemistry. "The Carioca," a dance number they performed for *Flying Down*... with the signature move of touching foreheads, became all the rage.

After the success of *Flying Down to Rio,* RKO quickly made big plans for their unexpected new assets. A string of successful film partnerships followed.

The Gay Divorcee (1934)

They started with *The Gay Divorcee* (1934). The movie was adapted from *The Gay Divorce* (1932), the show that Fred Astaire and Clair Luce had presented to roaring success on the stage years before.

For the film, the story is set in London where American dancer Guy Holden (played by Fred Astaire) meets and falls for another American, the elusive Mimi Glossop (played by Ginger Rogers). What the besotted Guy does not know is that Mimi is married – in town to end a neglectful marriage from a man who doesn't quite wish to let her go.

Plans are made to force her freedom, but a series of misunderstandings keep landing Guy and Mimi in each other's paths. Love grows, music is made, and of course – a whole lot of dancing is performed as Fred and Ginger glide along the ups and downs of the romantic storyline.

Ginger was not yet the gifted dancer she would later prove to be here, but she acted from the top of her head to the tips of her toes, her face and body conveying so many emotions that audiences were riveted to the pairing.

Their follow-up to *Flying Down to Rio* and their first movie together as dancing sweethearts of the screen was a major success, pleasing both critics and audiences alike. *The Gay Divorcee* even earned five Academy Award nominations, and won the first Oscar for Best Original Song in 1934.

Capitalizing on the delightful duo's chemistry, the film has a song and dance number for "The Continental" that spanned more than 17 minutes – a record that would only be beaten by *An American in Paris* (1951) more than a decade later.

With their successful film partnerships, it is no surprise that RKO wanted to keep churning out projects for the pair. But there was reportedly some resistance from none other than the two actors themselves!

Fred Astaire, who had already come from a famous duo owing to his years' long partnership with his older sister Adele, had just started to be his own act. He wasn't quite keen on being the half of another pair again. He was not looking for a steady partner.

Ginger he reportedly liked working with enough, but his reservations had nothing to do with her. He told his agent at the time that he was not necessarily disagreeable to a film with Rogers; he was opposed to the notion of being packaged as a duo. Astaire was actually open about his high regard for her professionalism, especially later in their lives. He even once said that after awhile, it seemed as if others who danced with him *"looked wrong."*

As for Ginger, she did not quite have the technical dance skills of Fred, who was also a punishing perfectionist. Stories abound of her doggedly working until her feet bled – a tireless professional fighting to keep up without crying or complaining, even after dozens of takes. It was physically rigorous, but that was not the obstacle to her wanting to be part of a musical duo with Astaire. She was an actress, and a serious one who did not want to be typecast.

But the lure of their popularity proved too much to resist, and film after successful film featuring the pair followed. RKO benefited of course, but so did the two stars. This was especially the case for Fred who, aside from being handsomely paid as an actor, also had a lot of weight to throw behind the scenes. He had creative say on the choreography and presentation of dance onscreen, and also landed enviable deals to share in film profits.

One of the landmarks of Fred Astaire's vision for how dance numbers should be seen in movies is to feature the actors fully, head-to-toe, preferably in a single take... a marked contrast from the kaleidoscopic spectacle of the popular and beloved Busby Berkeley musicals. Cinema legend thankfully had room for both styles.

Another consistent element of dance in Astaire films is its place within a story. He is said to have championed the use of onscreen dance only as it moves along the plot. There is also usually three dances: a solo, one with a comedic tone, and of course, one with romance.

Roberta (1935)

Like *The Gay Divorcee* (1934), the next film by the hit tandem came from the stage. *Roberta* (1935) came from Broadway, and RKO locked down its rights as another vehicle for Astaire and Rogers.

As a dancer named Huck and his old flame Lizzie, Astaire and Rogers landed another hit with this musical rom-com. They were one of two couples in the film, about finding love around the high-end Parisian dress shop, Roberta's. It features the timeless track, "Smoke Gets in Your Eyes," which Fred and Ginger dance along to in a flawless, breathtakingly elegant number.

Another highlight is an energetic tap dance by Astaire and Rogers for "I'll Be Hard to Handle." The chemistry between them is magical here, and their considerable skills were shown off alongside their irresistible sense of fun. Some of their whispers and laughter, it's been said, were even spontaneous. They had a great time, and it not only showed, the feeling was contagious.

Top Hat (1935)

The duo and RKO set the bar high with three hit pictures, but with their fourth, *Top Hat* (1935), they outdid themselves.

It was the first of their films that was penned just for them. With original tracks by Irving Berlin, and studio recordings of songs by Fred released simultaneously with the movie, they landed yet another hit film and Fred landed a few more hit songs, including the classic, "Cheek to Cheek."

Once again it is set in London, though the characters played by Astaire and Rogers are American. Fred is visiting musical revue star Jerry Travers, whose tap dancing bothers his hotel neighbor, Ginger Rogers' Dale Tremont. She may be infuriated with him but he immediately falls for her. Jerry pursues her but there's a case of mistaken identity as she believes him to be married and rebuffs his earnest advances. There is general chaos, love, and of course, exhilarating song and dance.

Particular standout moments include Fred's iconic solo, "Top Hat, White Tie and Tails;" and the sheer movie magic of Ginger Rogers' infamous feathered dress as they danced along to "Cheek to Cheek."

Used upon her insistence and reportedly standing firm against objections from Fred and the director, the costume tossed up feathers all over Fred's jacket and the set... but swayed with gorgeous, unforgettable movement.

Top Hat became the biggest movie of Astaire and Rogers for RKO, and it was the studio's top grosser for the 1930s. It also landed several Academy Award nominations, and is not only considered the best movie of the duo, it may be one of the best musicals ever made. It is yet another Ginger Rogers film to find its way into the National Film Registry.

Follow the Fleet (1936)

Unsurprisingly, another project followed and again one with Irving Berlin penned songs: *Follow the Fleet* (1936).

As before, several songs for the film were recorded by Fred and released at the same time as the film. Clever Mr. Astaire, however, had also included one of his own compositions, "I'm Building Up to an Awful Let-Down." Also as before? Both the songs and the films were hits!

The setting this time around is San Francisco, where sailor "Bake" Baker (Astaire) and his buddy, "Bilge" Smith, head off to the Paradise Club. There, they discover Bake's ex-flame and former dance partner Sherry (Rogers) is a performer.

Astaire and Rogers were one of two romantic pairs for the film, where Bilge builds a relationship with Sherry's sister, while Bake and Sherry find love anew.

Playing a couple with history, Astaire and Rogers showed off their storied chemistry in enviable banter and rapport. One of the highlights was Ginger's rare dance solo, for "Let Yourself Go."

Swing Time (1936)

The hits kept coming.

For *Swing Time* (1936), RKO brought back *Roberta* (1935) composer, Jerome Kern for Astaire and Rogers' sixth outing. As before, Fred recorded music for release along with the film. A standout track hit the top of the charts, won an Academy Award for Best Original Song, and is still a familiar and beloved piece of music after all these years: "The Way You Look Tonight."

In this film, Astaire plays dancer Lucky Garrett, who makes his way to New York to prove he's good enough to marry a girl back home. But in the City, he meets Penny Carroll (Rogers), a dance instructor who, after a few missteps, he connects with professionally and eventually, romantically. Lucky then has to reevaluate what he wants from his life and who he wants in it... ideally, before the attractive Penny marries her own secondary love interest.

Swing Time is widely considered a close second to *Top Hat* (1935), as the dancing duo's best film together. It may even surpass *Top Hat* for the caliber of dancing; one number for example, was the result of 47 takes in one day, and paid in part with Ginger's bloodied feet. Amazingly, she is believed to have still considered this her favorite of their partnerships.

Like *Top Hat*, this enduring musical is also in the National Film Registry for preservation.

Shall We Dance (1937)

For not-so-lucky number seven, RKO brought in the songwriting talents of the famous Gershwin brothers, George and Ira for *Shall We Dance* (1937).

Top Hat (1935) had set the high mark for the dancing pair's profitability. *Follow the Fleet* (1936) had also delivered revenues, but was less financially stellar due to costs. The film that followed it, *Swing Time* (1936) did well enough at the box office. *Shall We Dance*, however, did not quite fare as well as its predecessors, and was not as profitable.

It was their nth pairing in just a handful of years after all, following a tried and true formula that may have already been too well-worn for audiences at the time: boy meets girl, boy chases girl and woos her with song and dance, and shenanigans ensue around a loose plot. Production costs were also high.

But playing a ballet dancer (Astaire) and a musical revue star (Rogers) caught in a fake marriage, the pair still knew how to thrill their fans. The film's track, "They Can't Take That Away from Me" was also nominated for an Oscar.

A memorable highlight of the film was when the pair upped the ante in dancing and charmingly performed "Let's Call the Whole Thing Off" on roller skates.

Carefree (1938)

In their next film together, *Carefree* (1938), Fred Astaire's Dr. Tony Flagg has a big problem on his hands: his best friend's fiancée, radio singer Amanda Cooper (Ginger Rogers) keeps putting off the wedding. Tasked with psychoanalyzing her, his difficult job just gets even harder when they get off on the wrong foot, and then later, fall in love.

In real life, the pairing and its home studio were facing a dilemma too. They've seen a decline in reception and/or an increase in production costs to the duo's projects, which was making their brand of musicals less sustainable. There appeared to be a downward trajectory, and when *Carefree* came out, it had even failed to make money for RKO.

On a lighter note, it did get a number of Academy Award nominations and has a unique place in the story of Fred Astaire and Ginger Rogers. In the stunning dreamscape set for the number, "I Used to Be Colorblind," their moves were slowed down to breathtaking effect, and coupled with a sweeping score and ending with – that – kiss, they again made movie magic. It was the longest they locked lips onscreen; Fred was usually of the belief that dance was symbolic enough of romance.

Speaking of lips and kisses... loose lips around Hollywood had people saying that perhaps Fred and Ginger weren't getting along.

Speculation on the precise nature of their relationship was of course unavoidable because of the lengthy and generally successful partnership they shared. But while there was speculation they were romantically involved at some point, there was also growing speculation on whether they even liked working together at all!

As was mentioned earlier, there was some initial hesitation to the team up due to how it would impact their solo ambitions. But is it possible that over the course of working together, they also did not like each other?

In her later years, long after the height of the partnership, Ginger has been quoted as saying they *"were never bosom buddies..."* One biographer even remembered her referring to her former, frequent collaborator formally as "Mr. Astaire."

Whatever they may have had between them though, their best work was already behind them. It would all soon come to an end.

The Story of Vernon and Irene Castle (1939)

The pair's final outing with RKO as a duo came the following year, with something different from what they've done before.

Departing from their tried and tested screwball comedies, *The Story of Vernon and Irene Castle*

(1939) is based on the real life famous husband-and-wife pairing of ballroom.

One of the most remarkable stories about the making of this film, is a shot that took 54 takes to perfect... again at the cost or Ginger's bloodied feet, which are fabled to have streaked the floors through her shoes.

Unfortunately, perfection didn't equate to RKO making serious bank with the film, and Fred and Ginger's work as a pair for the studio ended with this sad tale. Fred Astaire and RKO parted ways afterwards too.

The lackluster performance of the film is widely regarded not as a failure of Astaire or Rogers though, but a reflection of the decline of the musical as a film genre.

Not that it mattered much to the legacy of Astaire and Rogers - already well-written at this point. With just nine films for RKO in less than a decade, Fred Astaire and Ginger Rogers had already cemented their Hollywood legend and place in American film history... and it all began unexpectedly with *Flying Down to Rio* (1933).

Interestingly, Ginger was not the only creative collaborator Fred found in that film. Behind the scenes, he connected with dancer / choreographer, Hermes Pan, who was assisting choreographer Dave Gould at the time. Astaire and Pan eventually worked on 17 films together – almost twice that of the number of films he had worked on with Ginger!

Another recurring, important figure in the Astaire / Rogers pairing is director Mark Sandrich. He was at the helm for several of their film outputs under RKO: *The Gay Divorce* (1934); *Top Hat* (1935); *Follow the Fleet* (1936); *Shall We Dance* (1937); *Carefree* (1938); and two Astaire films absent Ginger but with Bing Crosby, *Holiday Inn* (1942); and *Blue Skies* (1946), both with Irving Berlin's music and for Paramount.

Fred had another defining partnership behind-the-scenes.

People may have marveled at his chemistry with Ginger, and some people even harbored hopes that they had genuine romantic inclinations toward each other. But in real life, Fred Astaire was devoted to his wife, Phyllis.

Flying Solo

They may be best remembered as a pair, but both in the professional and personal sense, Fred Astaire and Ginger Rogers had full careers and lives well beyond each other.

The Barkleys of Broadway (1949)

From 1933 to 1939, they made nine pictures for RKO with outsize impact. They reunited ten years later for *The Barkleys of Broadway* (1949) with MGM, their only movie together in Technicolor.

Interestingly, Ginger was not the original lead for this film; it was supposed to be Judy Garland, ailing at the time. There are also reports of Fred hesitating with the project and his leading lady. He reportedly felt it was in some ways, a step back in their careers given everything they have achieved since their partnership a decade past.

Nevertheless, the project pushed through and according to the director, Charles Walters, his two stars were polite and professional. Not particularly warm or close, but they did whatever they had to do. Rumors of either romance or active dislike between them are unconfirmed, but it was clear they at least worked well together.

With *The Barkleys of Broadway* added into the mix, Fred and Ginger soared with ten films as a love team, with 33 paired dance routines. They set musical and dance trends, and gave audiences iconic numbers at almost every turn, right from "The Carioca" of their very first film.

From dancing with foreheads touching to dancing "Cheek to Cheek," they also playfully did "Waltz in Swing Time," tapped, foxtrotted and roller skated their way into the hearts of an America struggling in The Great Depression.

Looked at quantitatively though, their peak as a pair was just ten movies over barely more than a handful of years. The impact of their partnership is outsize, considering this was just a small window of time in the careers of two prolific, long-lived actors.

Going through each of their enviable, *separate* bodies of work, Fred Astaire and Ginger Rogers were so much more than the films they made together.

Ginger Without Fred

Ginger was a serious actress who did not want to be typecast. The Astaire partnerships may have cemented her Hollywood appeal, but they nevertheless also pushed her into certain formulas. Furthermore, she was treated as somewhat like the lesser half of the pair – and was compensated to reflect it.

She kept busy with many other projects (and other partners!) though, even at the height of the dancing duo's immense popularity. Some of her best work is actually sans Fred Astaire.

For *Stage Door* (1937), she shared top-billing with Katherine Hepburn as aspiring artists trying to find their big break while sharing a boarding house in New York. The stellar cast includes Lucille Ball and Oscar-nominated Andrea Leeds, in a film that was nominated for multiple Academy Awards including Best Picture.

The following year she shared the screen with James Stewart for *Vivacious Lady* (1938), about a professor and a singer managing the family fallout of their whirlwind romance. The film was nominated for two Oscars.

The RKO rom-com *Bachelor Mother* (1939), where she played a salesgirl mistaken for the unwed mom of an abandoned baby, was a hit. As was *The Major and the Minor* (1942), which was the first Hollywood film directed by the later legendary Billy Wilder, who also co-wrote it. This film is particularly a must-see for Ginger Rogers fans, because it is here that she shares the screen with her formidable mother, Lela Rogers.

The same year found her doing the title role for *Roxie Heart* (1942), which is based on the story of the popular play, *Chicago*. This sanitized, Production Code-compliant version is a beloved film for fans of Rogers, who was perfect as the wisecracking, saucy, opportunistic showgirl.

A decade later, she was the leading lady of Cary Grant for the beloved screwball comedy, *Monkey Business* (1952). They play a husband and wife hilariously finding youth anew.

Kitty Foyle (1940). Her most famous film without Astaire is probably the one that got her an Academy Award for Best Actress: the "woman's picture," *Kitty Foyle* (1940).

In this bittersweet drama, she plays the feisty title character, a secretary from a humble background who finds romance with her high society boss. Family pressure and social class differences send her away and into the path of a doctor. Her second chance at love, however, is threatened by the return of her irresistible first.

Rogers landed her Oscar with this tearjerker, controversially besting stiff competition from the likes of Bette Davis, Katherine Hepburn and Joan Fontaine. Naturally, she became amongst the most in-demand and highest paid actresses in town.

All good things come to an end though, and while Ginger Rogers continued to be a well-employed actress, she eventually had to give up leading lady status by the end of the 1950s.

She still appeared on films though, and also appeared frequently on television. Her final feature film was *Harlow* (1965), but she would have television credits going all the way up to the late 1980s.

She was a very hot ticket in the New York and London theaters too, doing long, hit runs of *Hello Dolly* on Broadway and *Mame* across the pond in the 1970s.

Savvy, tireless Ginger also had diverse revenue streams. She went on successful, worldwide nightclub tours. Aside from being in entertainment, during World War II she also had a ranch in Oregon that supplied milk to a nearby military camp. She became a spokesperson for JC Penney as well, and had a stint as a lingerie designer. She was also a champion for women's rights.

Her career in the late 1980s and early 1990s was the victory lap for a legendry actress at the end of a beautiful, well-sustained run. She released a hit autobiography in 1991, was an honoree at the Kennedy Center in 1992, and landed a Women's International Center Living Legend Award in 1995.

She passed away at the age of 83 that same year on the 25rh if April, from congestive heart failure.

Ginger's Partners

Fred Astaire was Ginger's most famous male partner in Hollywood, but she shared the screen with a lot of other legends throughout her enviable years in the industry spotlight, including Jimmy Stewart and Cary Grant as mentioned above, and Clint Eastwood in *The First Traveling Saleslady* (1956).

She had a number of real-life leading men too.

Jack Culpepper. Her first husband from when she was in her late-teens and before she found stardom in the stages of New York City was fellow vaudevillian, Jack Culpepper. They divorced in 1931.

Lew Ayres. Her husband during the heady days of her RKO musicals with Astaire was the actor Lew Ayres, famous for *All Quiet on the Western Front* (1930). They were married from 1934 to 1941, but had separated earlier in the late-1930s.

During the time of separation, Ginger is believed to have dated famous filmmaker / industrialist / aviator, Howard Hughes. He was allegedly unfaithful. But during the same period, she is also believed to have had a sporadic relationship with director George Stevens, with whom she worked on *Swing Time* (1936) and *Vivacious Lady* (1938).

Ginger is also believed to have been in a relationship with actor Cary Grant in the 1940s and / or the 1950s – they shared the screen for the films *Once Upon a Honeymoon* (1942) and *Monkey Business* (1952).

Jack Briggs. A few years after her marriage with Ayres officially ended, Ginger married a Marine named Jack Briggs in 1943. They met when she was on tour with the USO during the war. The couple parted ways in 1949.

Jacques Bergerac. In 1953, she married French actor, Jacques Bergerac. They were co-stars in *Twist of Fate / Beautiful Stranger* (1954). Husband #4 was younger than she was by 16 years. Unfortunately, the marriage ended after 4 years.

William Marshall. Later, she fell in love and took another plunge, with bandleader / actor / producer / director, William Marshall. They were married from 1961 to 1969.

Fred Without Ginger

Fred Astaire had a lot of solo work going for him too, even during the years of his and Ginger's partnership.

On his own, he was a hit-making recording star, with his accessible voice serenading the public with some of the most iconic pieces of music ever made.

For a while he also hosted a popular radio program called The Fred Astaire Show for the NBC network. It closed after one season, but only because Astaire strained having to juggle it with his film commitments as an actor and choreographer.

As early as 1937 – the same year as *Shall We Dance* – he was already in a film without Ginger: *A Damsel in Distress* with 18-year-old Joan Fontaine. It was only Fred's second film without Rogers, the first being his debut with Joan Crawford a few years earlier, in *Dancing Lady* (1933).

Fontaine and Crawford, who landed Academy Awards for their acting achievements in 1942 and 1945 respectively, were only two of the Golden Age legends who were lucky enough to have been Fred Astaire's dancing partner onscreen.

He appeared with stunner Paulette Goddard in *Second Chorus* (1940); and tore up the dance floor with one of the world's best tap dancers, Eleanor Powell in *Broadway Melody of 1940* (1940). Of this leading lady he was all praises, and had described her as being in *"a class by herself."*

He found a match with sizzling and talented Rita Hayworth (a scion of the famous Cansino family of dancers whom he met in his youth), for *You'll Never Get Rich* (1941) and *You Were Never Lovelier* (1942).

He was also great buddying it up with male stars like Bing Crosby for *Holiday Inn* (1942) and *Blue Skies* (1946); and with fellow legendary song-and-dance superstar and rival, Gene Kelly in the revue-style, *The Ziegfeld Follies* (1946). The same all-star film also found him partnered up with Cyd Charisse and Lucille Bremer (actresses he would work with again in later projects).

In 1946, he had a brief retirement from doing motion pictures, wherein he focused on other business ventures – he was involved in horse racing, and established a chain of dance studios.

But he had so much more to offer, and returned with a bang for *Easter Parade* (1948) with the legendary Judy Garland. He was a replacement for Gene Kelly, who was injured before production started. Fred's successful return yielded even more projects, including one with his old partner, Ginger Rogers for *The Barkleys of Broadway* (1949). He usually released hit soundtracks to go with his movies.

As an actor, singer, dancer and choreographer, Fred Astaire made a unique figure in Hollywood. He had plenty of achievements that were aligned to each other, but difficult to categorize. This made him difficult to honor in a conventional manner, though thankfully he did get a special Academy Award in 1950, for his artistic contributions.

His award was presented to him by his most famous "other half," Ginger Rogers. He was not physically present to receive the honor but had been available on a phone call to Hollywood from New York. Even when they were not in each other's immediate sphere, they had palpable rapport.

She opened formally with praises for his work, but was openly giddy when the phone call to Fred came through. He expressed his delight at the ward eloquently, and also thanked her for her graciousness adding, *"remember, I had a partner."* Without missing a beat she quipped, *"Thanks Fred but that's not what it says here on the Oscar,"* to the audience's laughter.

Their individual careers continued on. For Fred, more musicals and dancing partners followed into the 1950s, including Cyd Charisse for the massive hit, *The Band Wagon* (1953), and with such ingenues as French actress Leslie Caron for *Daddy Long Legs* (1955); and the lovely Audrey Hepburn for *Funny Face* (1957).

In the 1960s, most of his work was for hit music and for hit television appearances. He landed multiple Emmys for his work on specials like *An Evening With Fred Astaire* (1958) and *Astaire Time* (1960), and worked with several record labels to release songs and soundtracks, including his own, Ava Records.

He wasn't going to be the leading man forever but like Ginger he was tireless and able to find success in multiple media well into the 1970s: music, television, voice work for animation and of course, film. Fred even gave everyone welcome shocks for amazing acting roles that did not primarily involve music or dancing.

He wowed audiences for his work in *On the Beach* (1959), which landed him a Golden Globe nomination for Best Supporting Actor. He would take home the win for this same award over a decade later, for the mega-hit disaster movie, *The Towering Inferno* (1974). *The Towering Inferno* is also the only film that gave Astaire an Oscar nomination for his acting work.

His last movie musical was for Francis Ford Coppola's *Finian's Rainbow* (1968), though he continued to be a regular and beloved sighting in other film and television work after that.

In the final years of his career, he raked in more accolades for his legacy, including the Cecille B. DeMille Award at the Golden Globes in 1961; the first Kennedy Center Honors in 1978; and a Life Achievement Award from the American Film Institute in 1981.

His final appearance on the big screen was for *Ghost Story* in 1981. He passed away on the 22nd of June 1987 from pneumonia, at the age of 88. The Grammy Awards honored his contributions to music with a posthumous lifetime achievement award in 1989.

Fred Astaire in Love

In the decades after Fred Astaire's final RKO pairing with Ginger and until his death, he definitely made for himself an enviable career as a singer and actor, who was versatile enough to find success on his own or with different partners.

In real life though, for a long time there was only one girl for Mr. Astaire: the American socialite Phyllis Livingston Potter, who was Fred's first love.

While he may have entertained short-lived romantic interests before her (sporadic reports even claim he and Ginger Rogers dated briefly while they were on Broadway), Phyllis was the love of his life.

They met in 1931, during a golf luncheon in Long Island attended by socialites and other luminaries. Boston-born Phyllis was an American aristocrat, with family links to prominent figures in the fields of medicine, philanthropy, politics and finance. She made her debut in society in 1926 and later married a fellow-socialite, Eliphalet Nott Potter III. The marriage was short-lived and eventually dissolved, but had yielded a son named Peter.

Fred was charmed by her during that fateful 1931 meeting. Phyllis seemed to draw a lot of male attention though, and Fred Astaire had a lot of competition for the doll-like socialite.

Not a lot men had the assets Fred Astaire could draw upon, though. He had grace and elegance and hit theater shows he invited her to and impressed her with, of course. But he also had dogged determination, and the same pursuit of excellence he demanded of himself in his performances, he brought to bear on their courtship.

Phyllis was reluctant to enter another relationship after her first marriage soured, but after two years, Fred won her over.

Phyllis was a vital support to Fred in the months that followed the departure of his sister Adele from their duo act and her retirement from performing. Phyllis motivated him during *Gay Divorce* (1932), the show that firmly stamped his strength as a solo stage and recording star and the show that eventually lured in Hollywood interest.

They married in July 1933, just before Fred jetted off to Hollywood to pursue stardom on the silver screen. There, he worked on his film debut on loan to MGM, *Dancing Lady* (1933) with Joan Crawford and Clark Gable. It was soon followed by RKO's *Flying Down to Rio* (1933) for his first onscreen dance with Ginger Rogers... and the rest as they say, is history.

Between the end of filming *Flying Down to Rio* and the superstardom that followed though, Fred Astaire left the U.S. to do a limited run of *Gay Divorce* in London, where it was also a hit. It was his last work on the stage.

As mentioned earlier, the years after *Flying Down to Rio* were heady, and marked by the box office dominance of Fred Astaire and Ginger Rogers. Unfortunately though, it seemed as if the relationship between Fred's screen sweetheart and his wife was a little cold.

Phyllis was rumored to have been frosty with her husband's reel love, Whether it was driven by jealousy or simple personality differences is not known, but Ginger has been quoted as stating Phyllis never quite "*warmed up*" to her.

It may be recalled that *Carefree* (1938) had a drawn-out dance scene ending with a kiss. Fred was reserved about kissing leading ladies, relying more on the communication of dance. But it has also been speculated that his reserve may have been due at least in part to Phyllis not wanting her husband to lock lips with other women.

Fred and Phyllis had a strong relationship and they had two children together, Fred and Ava (the namesake of his record label). It was a loving marriage, and the loss of Phyllis from cancer in 1954 was devastating.

When Phyllis passed away, Fred was so heartbroken that he reportedly considered paying his way out of his commitment to *Daddy Long Legs* (1955). But he powered through not only for the film, but for decades more of work in the industry.

He even found love anew: on the 24th of June 1980, he married his second wife, jockey Robyn Smith. He was 81 years old and she, 35.

The Last Dance

The last movie of Fred Astaire and Ginger Rogers was in 1949, but their last public dance together was at the 1967 Academy Awards.

As presenters of one of the awards, they were introduced as the "*undisputed king and queen of Hollywood musicals.*" Already enthusiastically received by the audience upon their appearance, there was an audible rise in applause and energy when Fred gave his old partner a little twirl.

They still looked good together. Their bodies still knew each other. With their entwined hands, open arms, coordinated feet, big beautiful smiles and warm gazes, they still moved well together. There was still banter and cackling energy between them.

In just a few seconds, they gave the world one more peek at that lightning-in-a-bottle chemistry. No matter how they really felt or how they really operated behind the scenes, twenty years after the last film they did together and they still knew how to titillate their audience.

It was one of the happiest accidents of the world that they found each other. Fred was the polished, technically brilliant gentleman of the stage whose partner stepped away from the limelight at just the right time, leaving him to forge his own path. Plucky Ginger's star rose around the same period, and on her road as a more serious actress, took a detour down the road of romantic comedy musicals when she filled in for an actress who had vacated a role.

They stumbled into each other in a way, but landed securely into each others arms. They were in step with each other's strengths and weaknesses and together, they were in tune with the needs of the times.

They had full lives before each other, after each other, and beyond each other. But in just a few years of working together, they glided along to the undulations of the music of the fates, as they headed toward their destiny as two of Hollywood's brightest and most enduring stars.

Made in the USA
Columbia, SC
12 May 2020